Christmas Jubilation

8 SPARKLING SELECTIONS
FOR FLUTE & PIANO

ARRANGED BY
JUDY NISHIMURA

ISBN 978-1-4768-1259-5

GlorySound

A DIVISION OF SHAWNEE PRESS, INC.
EXCLUSIVELY DISTRIBUTED BY HAL LEONARD CORPORATION

Visit Shawnee Press Online at
www.shawneepress.com

CONTENTS

THE ANGEL GABRIEL DANCED
("The Angel Gabriel" with "Sing We Now of Christmas")

Based on Basque and French Carols
Arranged by Judy Nishimura

A COOL SILENT NIGHT

Based on an Austrian Carol
Arranged by Judy Nishimura

BLOOMING JOY

("Lo, How a Rose E'er Blooming" with "Jesu, Joy of Man's Desiring")

Based on a German Carol and a Melody by J.S. Bach
Arranged by Judy Nishimura

CRADLE SONG
(Away in a Manger)

Based on Melodies by William J. Kirkpatrick
and Felix Mendelssohn
Arranged by Judy Nishimura

Christmas Jubilation

8 Sparkling Selections for Flute & Piano

ARRANGED BY
Judy NISHIMURA

GlorySound

EXCLUSIVELY DISTRIBUTED BY

HAL•LEONARD®
CORPORATION

7777 W. BLUEMOUND RD. P.O. BOX 13819 MILWAUKEE, WI 53213

HL35028562

THE ANGEL GABRIEL DANCED

("The Angel Gabriel" with "Sing We Now of Christmas")

Flute

Based on Basque and French Carols
Arranged by Judy Nishimura

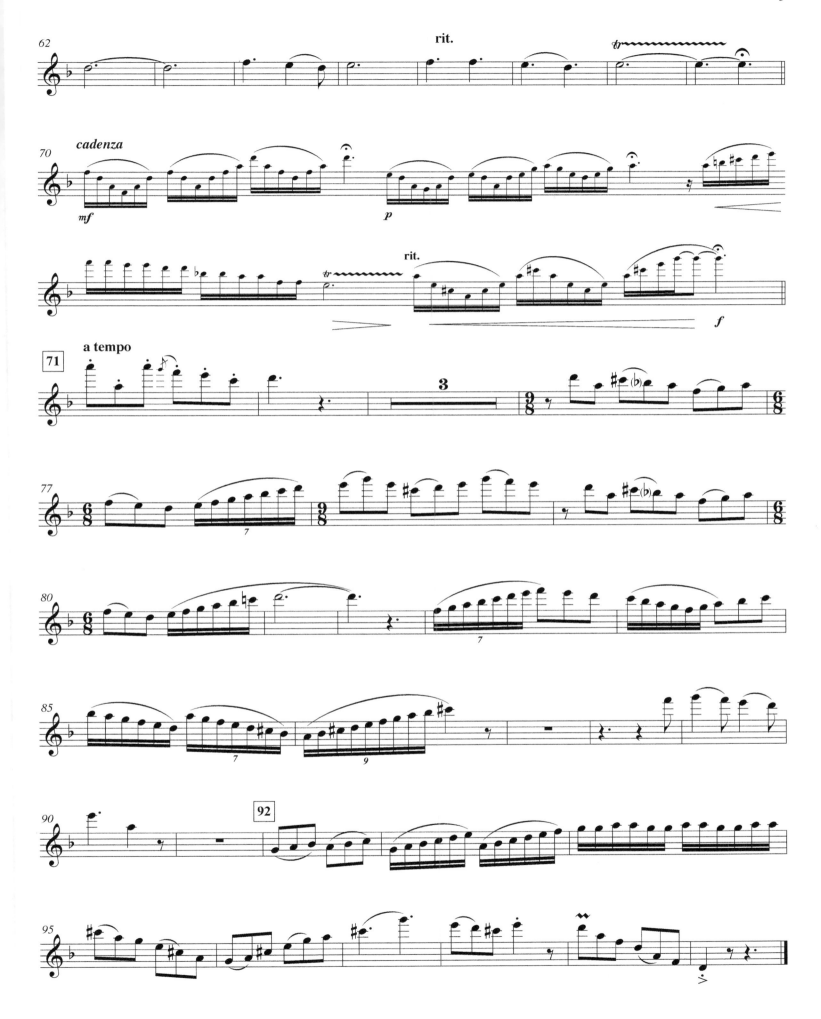

BLOOMING JOY

("Lo, How a Rose E'er Blooming" with "Jesu, Joy of Man's Desiring")

Flute

Based on a German Carol and a Melody by J.S. Bach
Arranged by Judy Nishimura

A COOL SILENT NIGHT

Flute

Based on an Austrian Carol
Arranged by Judy Nishimura

CRADLE SONG
(Away in a Manger)

Based on Melodies by William J. Kirkpatrick
and Felix Mendelssohn
Arranged by Judy Nishimura

Flute

WEAVING GREENSLEEVES
(What Child Is This?)
Three settings woven together

Flute

Based on an English Carol
Arranged by Judy Nishimura

MERRY ANGELS

("Angels We Have Heard on High" with "Ding Dong! Merrily on High!")

Flute

Based on French Carols
Arranged by Judy Nishimura

OH, JOY!
("Joy to the World" with "Ode to Joy")

Flute

Based on Melodies by George Frideric Handel
and Ludwig van Beethoven
Arranged by Judy Nishimura

14

A WINTER HOMECOMING
(In the Bleak Midwinter)

Flute

Based on Melodies by Gustav Holst and Antonín Dvořák
Arranged by Judy Nishimura

Also available:

O Holy Night
A Christmas Collection for Flute & Piano
Book/CD Pack
HL00842454

Christmas Carols – Flute
Book/CD Pack
HL00842132

Christmas Favorites – Flute
Book/CD Pack
HL00841964

Christmas Hits – Flute
Book/CD Pack
HL00842416

MERRY ANGELS
("Angels We Have Heard on High" with "Ding Dong! Merrily on High!")

Based on French Carols
Arranged by Judy Nishimura

WEAVING GREENSLEEVES
(What Child Is This?)

Three settings woven together

Based on an English Carol
Arranged by Judy Nishimura

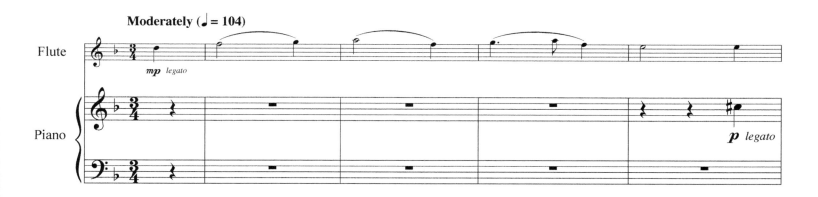

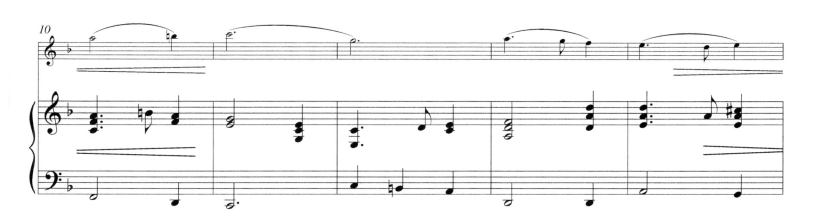

OH, JOY!
("Joy to the World" with "Ode to Joy")

Based on Melodies by George Frideric Handel
and Ludwig van Beethoven
Arranged by Judy Nishimura

A WINTER HOMECOMING
(In the Bleak Midwinter)

Based on Melodies by Gustav Holst and Antonín Dvořák
Arranged by Judy Nishimura